CHRISTMAS TREE

By Roger Mills

INSPIRED BY AN IDEA FROM SUSAN MILLS

First published 2020
© Jeremy Mills Publishing

ISBN: 978-1-911148-32-6

All rights reserved. No part of this book may be reproduced in any form or by any means without prior permission in writing from the publisher.

Dedicated to the immortal Chinese ginkgo tree
and to all who believe in magic.

CHAPTER ONE

November, late November. Very late November. Wet, wintry, water-logged, and wind-lashed November. Fell, foul November, Sou'wester-soaking, sullen, sodden, sodding bronchitis-bringer. No one likes November. But a bit of bad weather will put no stop to workings in the "Wild Wood".

* * *

The up-and-down-motor- mechanical pitch and the whine of puissant pruners from farmer Yabsley's workshops block-out softer sounds on this drenched, drenching, November morning. The men wear ear-defenders to muffle the noise and protect their eardrums from the decibel overdose.

"Good weather for ducks" says a farmhand. He laughs at his own joke.

This is farmer Yabsley's forest of firs and spruce: Arbor Vitae, Novdram, Imperial, Alta Spruce, Scots Pine, Nordmann, Fraser, Princess and Majestic. He is czar of all he surveys, knows every quirk in the book.

November is Jacob Yabsley's busiest and hardest time of the year. In November, he harvests his Christmas trees. Decades standing in wet socks in wet plantations in wet Novembers, attendant on wet Christmas trees has brought farmer Yabsley wealth, but not health. He suffers acute arthritis in his left knee.

Yabsley's team of fellers work up and down symmetrical rows of young trees, brandishing

CHAPTER ONE

their chain saws, like Lee-Enfields. Behind them are rows of stumps oozing a sappy fragrance from wounds that are sticky and sometimes terminal.

The decapitated evergreen crowns have fallen in a confused clatter and clutter of dust, creaks, squeaks, sighings and soughings and broken boughs. They lie in the mud like wounded Tommies at Passchendaele, waiting for the stretcher-bearers.

But the men are smiling and laughing today. Cracking jokes. They are happy to be working and working together, catching up with the news, working as a team. A family.

A week of seasonal piecework stretches ahead under their gang-master boss, Jacob Yabsley, a man they respect. Yabsley listens....unlike some.

The law allows Yabsley to hire and fire fellers. They wear bright yellow high-vis protective clothing, supplied by Yabsley. On the back of each gilet are the words 'DANGER FELLER'.

All Yabsley's men have a roof over their heads and a camp bed in what used to be the Ops room of RAF Leconfield. On 14th February 1945 the Lancasters took off from England's East coast to deliver a personal and deadly Valentine card from Bomber Harris to the city of Dresden. When the Lancasters returned with open bomb doors, the famous old city was ashes, obliterated in the firestorm.

* * *

Yabsley clucks over "his boys". He's like a mother hen. They tell him their secrets, as if he was a priest in his confessional, and they, penitents. He will write personal letters for his illiterates. Morale in Yabsley's workforce is high. "It's not rocket science..... just give 'em a bed, some grub

CHAPTER ONE

(nothing too fancy, mind), H&C running water and daytime TV to snooze off to", says Yabsley.

Everyone is fond of the old boy. Yabsley listens... He tells it as it is.... Unlike some....... Ferris Osgood for example.... Osgood's accommodation is a disgrace. He crams up to sixteen men into his foul-smelling dorms. A stench of syrupy green fungoid faeces pollutes the ablutions. Puddles of urine fester, un-mopped, malarial and viral.

Walls and ceilings are crawling with an unattractive and unhealthy excremental black mould. There are no lavatories, no latrines, no ventilation in Osgood's dorms. The Osgood family believes that "Lavs are for Sissies"

Osgood wonders why his men are always off sick.

Like Yabsley, Osgood is a gangmaster. He is also a legend in the "Wild Wood" for dodgy dealings. Osgood's felonies commence at check-in when he confiscates his workers' Passports. He says it's 'regs' and 'compulsory'.

To get them back, Osgood will expect to be paid. He pretends to be a Union man, but he's a blackleg and a scab. Somehow, he gets away with it....

* * *

The "Gastarbeiter" begin to arrive at Yabsley's plantation in early-November. By the end of the month there is not a country in Europe that has not supplied a mercenary or two to the ranks of Yabsley's army of fellers.

From his plantations arise a Babel of Europe's tongues: The harsh guttural of Dutch and German melts into the soft dentals and fricative consonants of Poland and Russia.

"Schnell, schnell", the workers cry. "Wesolych Swiat", the Polish riposte. "Joyeux Noel", cries a

CHAPTER ONE

French feller. And from the Fatherland, "Frohe Weihnachten", and "Schaslyvono Rizdva!",... the echo of a whisper from the remote blizzard-swept Ukrainian Steppe.......

But Georgian and Rumanian is spoken. A little Slovene, a smithereen of Slovak.

* * *

"Careful with them cutters", yells Yabsley across the human and mechanical rumpus.

"We don't want no accidents, today of all days. 'Tis treacherous under-foot up there in the spinney. I've told 'ee before what my dad used to say",

"Moving parts don't go,
 when there's rain and snow"

All the spruces and firs belong to Yabsley. They took root as saplings decades ago when these men were boys in short trousers. They were mulched and matured in one communal act of arboreal activity.

Of all the trees, the Norwegian pines are the Housewives' Choice, for they drop no pine-needles onto a brushed carpet. They are the priciest.

For them there is special treatment. Each is thrust into a revolving drum. It emerges at the drum's end parcelled into a skin-tight protective straitjacket of green plastic.

They are piled up in a stack by the spinney. Yabsley's dripping and mud-spattered Toyota stands by, its engine idling. They dare not switch the engine off. With damp everywhere, no ignition key is going to fire it up again.

※ ※ ※

From the valley below comes the pleasant sound of a male-voice choir. The tree-fellers are singing seasonal songs.

CHAPTER ONE

*"O Tannenbaum, O Tannenbaum,
Wie treu sind deine Blaetter."*
*"O Christmas tree, O Christmas tree,
How lovely are thy branches."*

Later the men will go shopping for Christmas Trees with the wages they have earned from Yabsley. They will buy atomisers and aerosols which spray silver pixie dust, aglint and aglitter, over the dark green boughs as they await transportation to the village.

Yabsley was examining the last tree quizzically. It was small and shapeless. Almost a dwarf pine. The other trees called this freak, 'Stompie'.

In all the years he had spent in the forests, Yabsley had never seen a tree quite like it. Whence it came he did not know. Neither genus nor species. He turned it this way and that. He turned it upside down. He smelled it, shook it and listened for a heartbeat. Then he shrugged his shoulders.

"Well, I suppose someone might buy yer", he said, casually.

He drop-kicked Stompie back into the skip with the others. Then from inside his waistcoat pocket, he took out his old fob watch.

"Time we were off, gennelmen!" he said.

Stompie lay on top of the pile with the other trees.

"Where are they taking us?" asked Stompie.

"You?........Nowhere", said Priscilla who was a rather haughty Christmas Tree. She thought herself quite Somebody.

Then Yabsley's driver slipped the Toyota into reverse and they began their cautious descent in first, down the slippery gradient (Danger Steep Hill 4:1) that led to the village.

The Toyota had already nearly come to grief three times, when, braking suddenly at "Elbow Corner", the driver lost control altogether and

CHAPTER ONE

slewed across the road. Trees were scattered everywhere. Stompie was catapulted into the vegetation that grew tall from the flooded ditches by the roadside.

"Buggeration! Bang goes my bonus", the driver cried in anguish.

It was getting dark by the time every tree was reloaded and the Toyota resumed its crawl down the slime-line, which led from the spinney to the village. In the confusion and in poor light, the driver failed to notice that several trees had gone AWOL. There was no sign of Stompie. Stompie had vanished.

CHRISTMAS TREE

CHAPTER TWO

"Stompie's Song",
"A mother, who called her son 'Stompie',
Was appalled when he looked like a donkey.
She went to the Doc's.
(She thought it was Pox.)
But the cause was his genes, which were wonky".

Stompie was hungry and lost. But there was no shortage of ditch-water, which contains all the nutrients a tree needs to grow and thrive. (predominantly nitrogen and phosphorus).

Already Stompie could feel subcutaneous 'prickings', which were the first stirrings of a green shoot and a new yellow tendril forcing itself through a vulnerable spot in his outer 'skin. It must mean that Stompie was alive.....somewhere.

"Priscilla's Song:"
"There once was a tree called Priscilla,
Who wanted to be a guerrilla.
She contacted 'Che',
"An expert", they say.
And now she's an X rated killer."

* * *

The grassy knoll, where the spinney meets "The Wild Wood" is an excellent vantage point from which to view Yabsley's plantation. The two men had been up there for at least an hour. One had a pair of binoculars. He continually panned over the same bed of firs and spruces, making a note of the quantity and quality of Yabsley's Christmas Trees.

CHAPTER TWO

His companion held a dictaphone. From time to time he pushed a 'record' button and spoke into it. When the two men were satisfied, they shook hands and drove off in opposite directions in expensive chauffeur-driven limousines.

* * *

Kokkola is a small town. Nothing much goes unnoticed there. Soon news of two deluxe limos on Yabsley's plantation reached the ears of local investigative journalist, Karl Lindenbrau.

Sensing something 'out of the ordinary', Lindenbrau immediately went under-cover, merging unnoticed into the background as he joined the workforce as just another worker. He made a note of everything he heard and saw.

"....them cars up spinney way yesterday?"......

"'A-U-S 1', weren't her?"

"A Mercedes, or a BMW or summat?" Came the reply.

A BMW with a personalised numberplate was a gift to a competent sleuth.

In no time Lindenbrau had tracked down and identified one of the two men as Jurgen Auslander. The second he identified by a process of elimination as Uwe Kinderbracht. They were regulars on local TV, and frequent contributors to the business section of Kokkola's influential daily, "Finanzen Heute".

"What can they be up to?" Lindenbrau decided to do a little more digging....and eavesdropping.

Auslander and Kinderbracht were both local celebs, both well-known as business rivals. But the tone of that day's edition of "Heute" had done a sprightly one eighty degree turn in their traditional hostile quadrille. A truce seems to have

CHAPTER TWO

broken out between the two business enemies. In its place an entente cordiale, and a concerted attack on Yabsley.

"Old-fashioned, old fogey, old school tie". Heute sneered in a vicious and mendacious editorial.

* * *

Following this assault, Yabsley sat slumped in his grandfather's rocking-chair next to the dying embers in his Aga. He was snoring slightly. "Finanzen Heute" lay in a sodden crumpled heap on the floor. His dog 'Charlie' had urinated on it.

"G'boy, Charlie. You piss on 'em all", said Yabsley.

Charlie wagged his tail.

But Jacob Yabsley was at the end of his tether. The thought of an approaching winter depressed him. Everywhere he looked there were problems.

It had cost him a small fortune to get the Expulsion Order ousting Ferris Osgood for somebody more suitable. Now he was running out of money....... and his arthritis was getting worse,...much.... much.....worse.

On top of all this, he had just learned that he was in the crosshairs of a press campaign, orchestrated by '"Finanzen Heute" ' and its odious Editor, no friend of Yabsley. Trouble lay ahead at every turn.

Of much greater concern to the old farmer was that he had no heir. What was going to happen to his plantation when he passed over to 'the other side'? "What you need is some sun, dear," said Rosa Yabsley. Rosa was anxious about her husband's health and state of mind. She gave Jacob a magazine that might give him some ideas. That night Yabsley sat at his cluttered, chaotic desk. He filled out a questionnaire and enclosed a cheque made out to 'Holidays of a Life-Time'.

He had decided on an action totally out of character. Un-Yableyesque. He would take Rosa's advice....

"Somewhere in The Med perhaps", he said to himself..." But whereabouts in the Med?...Yabsley had no idea.... Mykonos?... He knew nothing about places like Mykonos..., but he liked the picture on the front of the holiday brochure.

He liked the blue skies, and he liked the white-painted houses, and the windmills. There were no white-painted houses, no windmills in Kokkola.... In Kokkola the skies were always grey.....

Before he had second thoughts, Jacob Yabsley posted a letter booking a fortnight at a small taverna, chosen at random from 'Holidays of a Lifetime'. It sounded fun, it was cheap, and it was called 'Boyz will be Boyz'.

CHRISTMAS TREE

* * *

The sun was at its zenith as Jacob Yabsley's taxi drew up outside "Boyz will be Boyz". Attached to the flagpole fluttered a flag striped in all the colours of the rainbow. The young man at reception pushed the visitors' registration book towards Yabsley.

"Sign there, duckie", he said.

Although he did not know it, Yabsley had chosen to spend a fortnight at the gayest venue on the Greek islands,-the island of Mykonos.

CHAPTER THREE

"The song of the forest"
"Our forest grows poisons galore.
Digitalis, belladonna, and more.
The tally reaches thirty
With Manzanilla de la muerte,
And others too hot for the Law."

* * *

Many years have passed. "Stompie's" girth has thickened. The industrialization of forestry has proceeded at an astonishing rate.

In the old days it took over one hour to fell and strip a Christmas Tree. Today it takes less than one minute. But Yabsley cannot afford modern machinery. It is too expensive, and after the legal fees Yabsley has paid to get rid of Ferris Osgood, he has only a little money left.

Meanwhile what had started as a mild local interest in Stompie has grown exponentially. What could be fairly described as "Stompie-mania" now stalks the land. Crowds gather wherever Stompie goes. They line the streets and applaud as his cavalcade passes by.

People reach out to touch him as he processes through the high street. They want to tear strips off his clothing and preserve them like religious relics in a reliquary.

Details of his fairy-tale existence thrilled those used to following what went for 'interesting' in dreary, dull, drab Kokkola:

Stompie's miraculous escape from Yabsley's Toyota, and his re-birth endowed the town in a folk-lore all its own. People came from as far as

CHAPTER THREE

Finland, just to catch a glimpse of the local hero. and take some cuttings. When they got back home, they planted these in their gardens and allotments. Not a single cutting took root.

Above all, everyone wanted a selfie of themselves in an embrace with Stompie. These were not gullible ignoramuses, but serious professional men and women: academics and intellectuals, biologists and eminent arboriculturists from university departments and Institutes. These were the cream of the Establishment's intelligentsia.

What excited these highly qualified emeriti was the discovery, made at the Faculty of Biology at the University of Oulu, that the paper and newsprint produced from the pulping of "Stompie's" branches had special properties.

Anything printed on Stompie-generated paper or newsprint, produced art, literature and scientific research of the highest quality.

There was magic in Stompie's genetic make-up. He was unique. The wood obtained from his branches, pulped and rolled out into paper at the nearby paper mills, possessed creative powers. This was a huge scientific discovery with huge ramifications for the arts and sciences, and with a potential fully to be analysed and understood.

CHAPTER FOUR

Stompie's fame spread throughout the country. Late in March 2020 a personal letter with a Swedish postage stamp addressed to Yabsley arrived from the Alfred Nobel Institute of the Royal Swedish Academy of Sciences in Stockholm.

The letter told Yabsley that he had been elected winner of the 2019 Nobel Prize for Biology, along with Ling-Jun- Kong, Herbert Crezus, Agnieszka Goreka, Alexandra Urbanek, Rainer Dunk, and Tomasz Patnek. The prize was a gold medal and nearly a million dollars.

"Funny old world", said Rosa Yabsley. (She was reading the Gazeteer of Helsinki University).

"Look at this. The prize for biology 2018 went to Roger Meusset and Bourras Benguida, for measuring the scrotal temperature asymmetry in naked and clothed postmen in France. Sounds a bit like your pals on Mykonos."

Jacob Yabsley winced, as he recalled the lovely island of Mykonos….all those young men with not a stitch on, mincing around hand-in-hand, making sheep's eyes at one another.

Yabsley got out his old suit, and gave it to Rosa to darn and clean (He had worn it last at his wedding to Rosa, and he had long since grown out of it. He accepted the medal, the money, and a five-course formal dinner in one of the best hotels in Stockholm, the Radisson Blu Waterfront.

There he was the centre of attention and admiration. The guests begged for any spare wood-pulp Stompie might have.

CHAPTER FOUR

But Yabsley's success was not welcomed by all.

Smarting from his humiliation in the Courts, Ferris Osgood thought only of revenge and the total annihilation of everything his foe Joseph Yabsley, had achieved.

FERRIS OSGOOD'S *Song*
"Debauched and lustful, gross and rude,
Leprous, scabrous, whorish, crude,
I love everything that's mean,
Horrid, torrid, or, obscene...."

CHRISTMAS TREE

CHAPTER FIVE

"The Great Fire of Kokkola" had started as a tiny spark from Osgood's cigarette lighter. Within an hour a tiny spark had become an uncontrollable inferno. By the time the Kokkola Urban Fire-Fighters arrived, there was nothing left for them to put out. Generations of meticulous arboriculture had gone up in smoke.

People died in the flames, and a fund was set up to commemorate Yabsley and his plantations. Those who saw Stompie die testified that he had disappeared in a green cloud accompanied by a heart-rending groan. It reminded the pious church-goers of Kokkola of the transfiguration of Elijah in the Old Testament at 2 Kings 2.11.

CHRISTMAS TREE

* * *

Rosa was left a rich widow. As Yabsley had no heir, his fortune went to her: the million-dollar prize from Alfred Nobel plus all the extras that fame had brought to the Yabsleys. (Rosa was in demand as a speaker on the lecture circuit. Her subject "Living with a genius").

With her bequest Rosa purchased a picturesque fisherman's cottage by the Aegean Sea on the island of Mykonos.

She enjoys watching the lithe, tanned, naked, ephebes cavorting playfully in the sea, as she breakfasts on new croissants straight out of the village bakery, with butter and honey from Greek bees. Would it be too 'forward' to invite one of the boys to breakfast?, she wonders.

CHAPTER FIVE

ROSA's Song
"I watch the boys naked and gay
Laughing with joy as they play.
They don't give a damn
for a fiftyish ma'am
How I long to join in their display."

Of the others, Osgood was handed a life sentence without parole for attempted murder. Priscilla was lost in the blaze. The two businessmen, Jurgen Auslander and Uwe Kinderbracht were fined heavily for attempted fraud, embezzlement, and forgery of an official document from the Kokkola Land Registry. The judge commended the evidence provided by the undercover detective, Kurt Lindenbrau, whose testimony in court contributed so much to the businessmens' conviction. The Editor of "Finanzen Heute" was sacked.

Yabsley's plantations were put on the market and snapped up for next to nothing by the 'big boys', West Fraser and Weyerhaeuser........ The money they spent was cash down the drain, all wasted.

The Yabsley plantations were barren.

Aerial footage shot from a drone shows a large unsightly brown patch where Yabsley's green plantations once flourished.

A visitor to the spot where these Christmas Trees once thrived, will see very little. Just ashes and mud.

But close to the trig point that marks the highest altitude in the area ,and placed where the spinny meets the "Wild Wood", there is a commemorative granite slab bought by the townsfolk of Kokkola. On it is carved:

CHAPTER FIVE

"In memoriam Jacob Yabsley (1936–2020), who brought magic to the hills and dales of Kokkola in the form of Christmas Trees. He was their master and they were his masterpiece."

Kokkola has become a place of pilgrimage. On November 22nd each year, thousands of believers in the existence and power of magic descend on Kokkola's smart, newly built B&Bs and guest houses.

Kokkola has become a tourist attraction and destination. The visitors walk from the accommodation they have booked in the village up past the spinney and the "Wild Wood" to the scene of the fire to lay flowers on Jacob Yabsley's memorial tablet. Each carries the bough of a Christmas tree, and they sing in unison the Christmas Tree hymn, "Tannenbaum", followed by Jacob Yabsley's own hymn.

JACOB YABSLEY'S SONG:
"The love of my life is destroyed.
Its end gives me grief unalloyed.
As the flames of that fire
Leapt higher and higher,
I mourned an unbridgeable void."

CHAPTER FIVE

CHRISTMAS TREE

www.ingramcontent.com/pod-product-compliance
Lightning Source LLC
Chambersburg PA
CBHW070803050426
42452CB00012B/2475